BEAUTY HACKS

FASHION HACKS

YOUR FASHION FAILURES SOLVED!

BY REBECCA RISSMAN

CAPSTONE PRESS
a capstone imprint

Savvy Books are published by Capstone Press,
1710 Roe Crest Drive, North Mankato,
Minnesota 56003
www.mycapstone.com

Library of Congress Cataloging-in-Publication Data
Library of Congress Cataloging-in-Publication data is
available on the Library of Congress website.
ISBN 978-1-5157-6827-2 (library binding)
ISBN 978-1-5157-6831-9 (eBook PDF)

Editorial Credits
Mandy Robbins, editor; Aruna Rangarajan, designer;
Kelli Lageson and Morgan Walters, media researchers;
Kathy McColley, production specialist

Photo Credits
All photos by Capstone Studio: Karon Dubke, except:
Amy Mokris, 48 (inset); Capstone Press: Aruna
Rangarajan, 29 (top); iStockphoto: izusek, cover;
Shutterstock: Africa Studio, 25, 42, Alena Ozerova,
43, andersphoto, 12 (middle), Andriy-Chik, 2, 46
(top), 48 (background), avs, 33 (scarf), AXL, 11
(bottom), bogdandimages, 30 (background), Dean
Drobot, 12 (background), 20, 28, Denys Kurbatov, 7
(bottom), Didecs, cover (back cover top left and top
right), Dragon Images, 16 (background), elenabo,
40 (top), FabrikaSmif, cover (back cover bottom
right), Jahina_Photography, 31 (middle), Kateryna
Yakovlieva, 23 (top left), Lana Smirnova, cover (back
cover bottom left), lkoimages, 33 (middle right), Lucy
Liu, 33 (dress), Marisa Lia, 33 (top right), Markevich
Maria, 29 (bottom), mimagephotography, 41 (bottom),
NinaMalyna, 34, NYS, 33 (sweater), octographer, 35
(middle), Olga Koval, 35 (bottom), photka, 9 (top
right), Picsfive, 35 (top), pzAxe, 23 (background),
solominviktor, 4, SunCity, 6, Syda Productions,
32, Tracy ben, 36 (top), vipman, 23 (top right),
wavebreakmedia, 47 (bottom)

Design elements: Shutterstock

Printed and bound in the USA.
082017   010695R

TABLE OF CONTENTS

INTRODUCTION

FASHION FIXES
FOR YOU

YOU KNOW THAT FEELING...

You're walking into school and feeling great. Suddenly you notice you're sporting a fashion disaster! Whether it's a broken flip-flop or a ripped shirt, you need to think on your fashionable toes, and fast.

After learning a few fashion hacks, any girl can handle an outfit "oops" like a pro. This book will teach you how to salvage a stained shirt, resize a dress at the last minute, and sew on a button — all while letting your inner beauty shine!

A FEW BASIC SUPPLIES NEEDED

* dryer sheets
* baby powder
* toothpaste
* glass cleaner
* zip-top bags
* needle and thread
* scissors

Remember To Be Yourself!

World famous fashion designer **Gianni Versace** once said,

Don't be into trends. Don't make fashion own you, but you decide what you are, what you want to express by the way you dress and the way you live.

He was emphasizing that fashion should not define anyone. Instead, it should **highlight who you already are.**

New shoes are always exciting — unless you slip them on and realize they are too tight. If you can't return them to the store, don't panic. There are fashion fixes that will save your soles.

CHAPTER 1
SHOES BLUES

TIGHT SHOES

Tight shoes can often be slowly and gently stretched to better fit your feet. You can do this simply by wearing them for a few days. But you might wind up with painful blisters.

If you only have a few minutes, try this hack.

Step 1 Put on a pair or two of thick, fuzzy socks.

Step 2 Slip your tight shoes on over them.

Step 3 Use your blow dryer to warm your shoes for two to three minutes. Keep your shoes and socks on for a few more minutes until they have fully cooled. Doing this will gently stretch the material of your shoes.

If you don't need to wear your shoes for a day or so, try this hack.

Step 1 Fill two large plastic zipper bags with just enough water to fit each bag into one of your shoes.

Step 2 Seal the bags tightly before placing them inside your shoes.

Step 3 Stick your shoes in the freezer. As the water freezes, the bags will slowly expand. Doing this will stretch your shoes into a more comfortable shape without harming the material of the shoes. Just a tip — you probably want to put your shoes in a grocery bag before you throw them next to the popsicles.

WHEN TO SHOE SHOP

Your feet swell during the day. To make sure you're buying shoes that will fit your feet no matter what time it is, go shoe shopping in the afternoon or evening.

FIX THAT FUNKY
FOOTWEAR

What's that smell? Are stinky shoes spoiling your style? Stay calm! You can hack your way to odorless kicks.

When you wear shoes, your feet sweat. Tiny bacteria feed off the moisture and create a nasty odor. To keep your shoes odor-free, you need to eliminate bacteria. The best way to do this is to keep it from growing in the first place.

STOP THE STINK BEFORE IT STARTS!

Remember these tips to keep your footwear fresh.

1. Wash your feet every day with antibacterial soap.

2. Wear clean socks every day. Change into clean ones if your feet get sweaty.

3. Do not wear the same shoes every day. Giving your shoes a break is a good way to keep bacteria from taking over.

STINKY SHOE SOLUTION

If your shoes already smell, try this quick hack. Many types of bacteria can't survive in freezing temperatures. By sticking your stinkers in the freezer, you'll kill many of the bacteria that cause odors.

WHAT YOU NEED:

wet
towel

+

stinky
shoes

+

large plastic
bag

WHAT TO DO:

Step 1 Use a wet towel to wipe down the outside of your shoes. Make sure to get them as clean as possible.

Step 2 Put your shoes inside a large plastic bag and close it securely. This will keep your shoes from stinking up your freezer.

Step 3 Place the bag in the freezer for 24 to 48 hours.

Step 4 Allow shoes to warm to room temperature before you wear them.

FOOTWEAR FIXES

Broken shoes are such a bummer. Luckily, you're a smart girl who can fix your footwear. Try these quick solutions to common shoe issues.

FRAYED SHOELACE

If the end of your shoelace is too frayed to thread through the holes in your shoe, don't toss it. Try this hack to extend the life of your laces.

WHAT YOU NEED:

frayed shoelace

+

craft glue

+

sewing thread (about an arm's length)

+

scissors

+

paintbrush

WHAT TO DO:

Step 1 Dip the frayed end of the shoelace into the craft glue. Make sure all the loose threads get a little glue on them.

Step 2 Pinch one end of the thread and the shoelace about a finger's width away from the frayed end.

Step 3 Tightly wrap the thread around the end of the shoelace. Start at your fingertip and wind the thread to the end of the frayed shoelace and back.

Step 4 Tie both loose ends of the thread around the lace and into a knot.

Step 5 Use the paintbrush to lightly coat the wrapped end of the shoelace in more craft glue.

Step 6 Let the glue dry. Snip the end of the lace so that it is neat and even.

BROKEN FLIP-FLOP

Flip-flops are awesome. They're comfortable, easy to slip on, and they go with just about anything. But flip-flops can be flimsy. Try this hack the next time your flip-flop breaks so that you don't wind up walking home barefoot!

WHAT YOU NEED:

broken
flip-flop

paper
clip

 +

WHAT TO DO:

Push the flip-flop strap through the hole in the sole. Loop the paperclip around the strap between the bottom of the flip-flop strap and the sole of the flip-flop. Test it out by gently tugging on the flip-flop straps from the other side. Put the shoe back on and be on your way.

Tip: This flip-flop fix won't last forever, but it will help you get by until you can change your shoes.

Get a
GRIP

Shoes can be frustrating. Sometimes you find the perfect pair for a dance or school event. You buy them, bring them home, and try them on one more time. Then you step onto a slick floor, and whoops! You find yourself flat on the floor.

1.

Wear your new shoes out on a rough surface, such as concrete or gravel. Not only will this help scuff up the soles to give you better traction, it will also help wear in your shoes so that they are more comfortable.

3.

Do you have any puffy paint in your craft bin? Paint some on the soles of your shoes. It will give your soles a nice, sticky surface to grip the ground. If you're feeling creative, you can paint a fun pattern or picture on the soles.

2.

If you don't have time to go on a gravel hike, just sandpaper the soles.

Silence the
SQUEAK

Are squeaky shoes sending the wrong message? If your shoes are speaking louder than you are, try this tip. Lift the insole away from the bottom of the shoe and sprinkle a little baby powder underneath. This will help stop your shoes from squeaking. As an added bonus, it will keep your shoes smelling fresh.

RENEW THOSE SHOES

Are your dress shoes looking a little dumpy? Add a little flair to old footwear. Try these fun tricks to cover scuffs and scrapes. You may just fall in love with your shoes all over again.

▶ ADD SOME SPARKLE

WHAT YOU NEED:

paper towel

water or glass cleaner

craft glue

small paintbrushes

crystals

WHAT TO DO:

Step 1 Wipe the surface of your shoes clean with a damp paper towel. If the shoes are patent leather, use window cleaner instead of water.

Step 2 Use a small paintbrush to apply craft glue to the back of your crystals.

Step 3 Apply crystals in a pattern along the heel, toe, or arch of the shoes.

Step 4 Let the glue dry completely before wearing your shoes.

▶ ADD A STRAP

WHAT YOU NEED:

old shoes  + glue gun and glue +  scissors + decorative ribbon

WHAT TO DO:

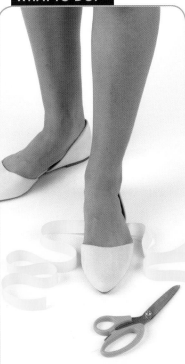

Step 2 Use your glue gun to secure a strip of ribbon along the bottom of the inside of the shoe. Leave plenty of extra ribbon on each side.

Step 1 Measure the length of decorative ribbon you need. Do this by putting on the shoe and draping the ribbon in different ways, either behind your heel and around your ankle or under your arch and up around your ankle. Cut the ribbon with plenty to spare on each side.

Step 3 Now it's time to have fun! You could simply tie the ribbon in front of your foot for a pretty accent. If you want to add an extra touch, cross it in front of your foot. Then loop it around the back of your ankle before tying a bow on top of your foot.

CHAPTER 2

LAUNDRY TIPS

LIPSTICK STAINS

Lipstick stains look scary, but they are usually easy to fix. Try this hack to save your favorite clothes from lipstick smudges.

WHAT YOU NEED:

hair spray   clean rag   warm water

+   +

WHAT TO DO:

Step 1 Spray hair spray over the stain.

Step 2 Let the hair spray sit for 15 to 20 minutes.

Step 3 Dip the clean rag in warm water and gently wipe away as much of the stain as you can.

Step 4 Wash the item as usual.

DEODORANT STREAKS

Have you ever pulled on a dark-colored shirt and then realized that you got white deodorant streaks all over it? Don't panic. Try these disappearing deodorant tips.

▶ Rub the stain with a pair of light-wash jeans.

▶ Pull the foam cover off of a wire hanger and use it to gently rub away the stain.

▶ Use a dryer sheet to gently rub away the deodorant stain.

OIL STAINS

Oily stains can be such a pain. One drop of salad dressing can ruin a favorite item. If you get something oily on your clothes, try one of these quick fixes.

▶ Apply a drop of color-free dish soap to the stain. Let it sit for a few minutes. Then gently rub with a damp cloth.

▶ Cover the stain in baby powder. Let it sit overnight. Dust it off, and then wash it as usual.

▶ Apply a little white vinegar onto a clean cloth and use it to dab away at the stain.

▶ Find a piece of white chalk. Using a clean napkin, blot away as much of the grease as you can. Then rub white chalk all over the stain. When you get home, toss the garment into the laundry, and wash it as usual.

▶ Oil stains don't have to be the end of your favorite leather items either. Try this the next time you dribble something greasy onto your leather bag, belt, or jacket. Sprinkle cornstarch onto the stain, and let it sit for about 30 minutes. Then dust off the cornstarch, and gently wipe away any excess with a dry rag.

BYE-BYE, WRINKLES!

Wrinkles can make your outfit look sloppy. But creases in your clothes don't have to wreck your look. A few easy hacks can keep you looking smooth.

▶ Hang your outfit in the bathroom while you shower. The steam from the hot water will gently relax the wrinkles in your clothes. If they aren't perfectly wrinkle free when you step out of the shower, coax them along by giving them a little tug in each direction.

▶ Use your flat iron to spot-iron wrinkles in your collar or hem. Just don't attempt this while you're wearing the wrinkled item. No need to burn yourself!

▶ Use a spray bottle to spritz a little clean water onto the wrinkles. Then shake the fabric and hang it up to allow the wrinkles to naturally fall out of the fabric.

▶ Toss your wrinkled clothes into the dryer with a wet washcloth for 10 minutes.

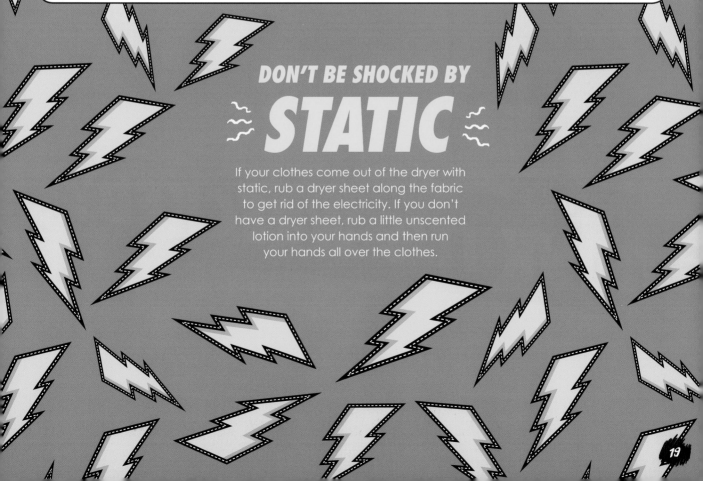

DON'T BE SHOCKED BY
STATIC

If your clothes come out of the dryer with static, rub a dryer sheet along the fabric to get rid of the electricity. If you don't have a dryer sheet, rub a little unscented lotion into your hands and then run your hands all over the clothes.

Did you snag your favorite shirt? Rip those awesome jeans? Does a broken zipper have you down? Don't be so quick to toss your clothes. Fashion hacks can save your favorite imperfect items.

CHAPTER 3

THINK IT'S WRECKED? THINK AGAIN!

QUICK SNAG SAVES

Some fabrics are very delicate. Silk, chiffon, lace, and other fine fabrics often look and feel amazing, but they don't always stand up to wear and tear. Have you ever accidentally snagged a beloved shirt and then gasped when you saw the damage? Don't worry. Try this quick save.

▶ Gently tug at the fabric surrounding the snag in all directions. This will help gently coax the snagged thread back into place. Just remember not to pull on the snag itself!

Sometimes your fabric won't get a jagged snag. Instead, you'll just notice a long thread hanging out. Whatever you do, resist the urge to pull on the thread. You'll just create a bigger problem. Don't snip the thread either. This will cause a hole to form. Try this instead.

WHAT YOU NEED:

snagged clothing

+

needle and thread

WHAT TO DO:

Step 1 Thread your needle.

Step 2 Pull the needle and thread through the center of the snagged string.

Step 3 Tie the thread into a knot at the end of the snagged string. (A)

Step 4 Pull the needle through the base of the snag. (B)

Step 5 Pull the snag through the fabric.

Step 6 Snip the thread. Do not snip the snag! (C)

A

B

C

TIGHTS CATASTROPHE

The next time you get a run in your tights, try this quick fix. Paint a little clear nail polish at the top and bottom of the run. If you're on the go, you can do this directly onto your tights while you're wearing them.

No More Snags

If you're constantly snagging your tights when you put them on, try taking off all your jewelry before putting on tights. If you're putting on especially sheer or delicate tights, wear a thin pair of gloves while pulling them on.

BUTTON BLUES

If you notice a button is barely hanging on, act fast. Apply a little clear nail polish over the fraying threads to keep the button on until you can get home. Then you can sew the button back on securely.

WHAT YOU NEED:

needle and thread +  scissors + button + toothpick

WHAT TO DO:

Step 1 Cut about an arm's length of thread off the spool. Press one end of the thread into the eye of the needle and pull it through.

Step 2 Tie the two ends of the thread into a knot.

Step 3 Stick the needle through the fabric from the underside, and sew a tiny X where you want your button to be anchored.

Step 4 Place your button on top of the X, and pierce the fabric from below it to bring your needle through one hole.

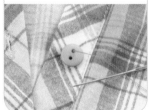

Step 5 Place a toothpick across the button. Pull the needle through the hole until you feel the knot at the back of the fabric. Bring the thread across the toothpick and then poke the needle down through the opposite hole. This will keep the button from sitting too close to the fabric. If you forget this step, your button will be too close to the fabric and it will be very hard to pull it through the buttonhole.

Step 6 Repeat Step 5 five to 10 times. End with the thread poking out on the underside of the fabric.

Step 7 Sew another tiny X, and send your needle through the loop from your last stitch to create a knot. Then take the toothpick out.

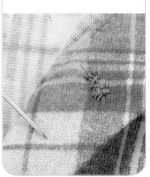

ZIP IT UP

Sticky zippers don't have to slow you down. Unstick the teeth by rubbing any of the following items along the zipper:

CLEAR LIP GLOSS

THE TIP OF A GRAPHITE PENCIL

PETROLEUM JELLY

BABY OIL

Turn a RIPPED SHIRT into a VINTAGE FIND

A torn collar, sleeve, or hem on a new shirt can be a total bummer. But a tear on a vintage shirt adds character. Turn your torn items into vintage finds with this simple salt-water hack.

WHAT YOU NEED:

1 cup salt

+

1 large bowl warm water

WHAT TO DO:

Step 1 Fill the bowl with warm water.

Step 2 Pour in the salt and stir to mix.

Step 3 Soak the ripped shirt in the salt water for three days.

Step 4 Remove shirt, rinse, and then wash as usual.

BEFORE

AFTER

24

Give Old Clothes New Life

If your old cotton T-shirt has a ripped or stained sleeve, don't toss it into the donation pile just yet. Instead, break out your scissors and get creative. Try cutting off the sleeves and collar to turn it into a tank top. Or cut a thick strip straight across the midsection to create a wide eternity scarf.

DYE DIY

If your favorite item is looking faded, stained, or just slightly sad, try something bold to give it new life. Head to the fabric store and buy some fabric dye. If you're feeling dramatic, dye the whole item a brand-new color.

OMBRÉ DYE

When people talk about an ombré effect, they're referring to a look where one color or shade fades into the next. This hot look can be done with hair color, nail polish, and even clothing. Try this cool technique to get an ombré effect on an old shirt.

WHAT YOU NEED:

fabric dye   large bowl   hanger

 + +

WHAT TO DO:

Step 1 Read the directions carefully on the fabric dye. Prepare a large bowl of the dye. Make sure your shirt is clean and prepared according to the dye's directions.

Step 2 Hang the clean shirt on a hanger. Hold onto the hanger and lower the bottom few inches of the shirt into the dye. Leave it there for 10 minutes.

Step 3 Hold onto the hanger and lower the shirt a few more inches into the dye. Leave it there for 10 minutes.

Step 4 Lower the shirt further into the dye. Allow it to soak for five more minutes.

Step 5 Lower the remaining fabric into the dye for just a few seconds.

Step 6 Hang the shirt to dry allowing any excess dye to drip down. This step is best done outside to keep from staining the floor.

TIE-DYE LEGGINGS

Patterned leggings are a great way to punch up your fall wardrobe. The next time your old leggings are looking a little faded, try this trick to get runway style. This hack works best on light-colored fabric.

WHAT YOU NEED:

fabric dye   + large bowl   + rubber bands

WHAT TO DO:

Step 1 Choose a dark-colored dye, such as black or navy. Carefully read the directions on the fabric dye. Prepare a large bowl of the dye. Make sure your old leggings are clean and prepared according to the dye's directions.

Step 2 Twist the legs of your leggings into long, tight ropes.

Step 4 Soak the leggings according to the directions on the fabric dye.

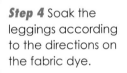

Step 3 Tie rubber bands every 2 to 3 inches (5 to 7 centimeters) up the leggings to create a striped pattern.

Step 5 Use scissors to cut the rubber bands off the leggings.

Step 6 Rinse and wash before wearing.

CHAPTER 4

GET THE RIGHT FIT

Clothes look their best when they fit well. They are also more comfortable. But sometimes a girl has to get creative to get the right fit. Try these hacks the next time your clothes aren't quite the right size.

KNOTS TO THE RESCUE

Knotting your clothes is a great way to make them shorter, tighter, or just more interesting. Add a low front knot to a shirt that is too long or loose. Try a knee-height knot on an oversized maxi skirt. Highlight your waist by knotting the bottom of a baggy button-down shirt to shorten it.

FROM SHAPELESS TO SHAPELY

Do you have a loose, shapeless top in your closet that seems too big to wear? Take that top out of retirement. These hacks will turn it into a fabulous statement piece.

▶ Wear the loose top over fitted jeans or leggings, and add a cropped jacket. The jacket will add structure and shape.

▶ Wear a thin leather belt over the shirt, just above where your bellybutton is.

▶ Tuck the top into a high-waisted skirt or pair of pants.

▶ If the shirt is long enough, wear it as a shirtdress over tights and boots. Add a faux fur vest for extra style points.

SUPER SAFETY PINS

Is your neckline too low? Is your strapless dress sliding down? Are the straps of your tank top too long? Before you pop those clothes in the donation pile, try a few safety pin tricks to get a good fit and a great look.

RE-WRAP YOUR DRESS

Wrap dresses and tops are comfy and stylish. But sometimes they're a bit too low cut for comfort. If your neckline is plunging lower than you'd like, pinch the fabric together where you want it to stay and use a safety pin to hold it in place. Then take the top or dress off and turn it inside out. Switch the safety pin from the outside to the inside. Try to keep the pin inside the seam, or camouflage it with a scarf or a broach.

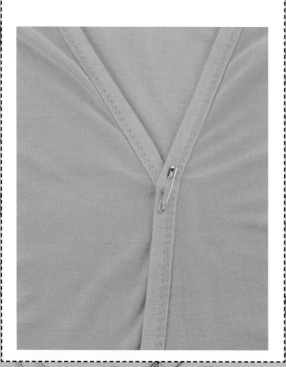

SAFETY STRAP

If your tank top or dress straps are too long, take it off and turn it inside out. Lay the item with the back side up. Pinch a couple fingers' width of each strap at the base. Fold the pinched straps down onto the fabric and safety pin them in place. Then try on the item and see if you've got the right fit.

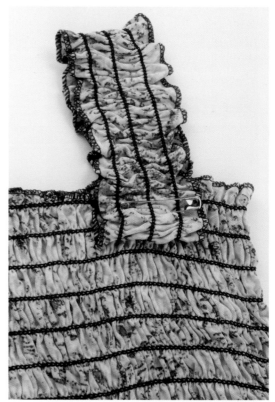

STRAPLESS SAVE

If your strapless shirt or dress doesn't feel snug enough, take it off and turn it inside out. Pinch a bit of fabric together, and safety pin it so that the pin is parallel to the seam. Turn the item right-side-out again, and put it on. Experiment with the safety pin to get the right fit.

RUBBER BAND TO THE RESCUE

Tight jeans can be such a pain! If they're a little tight around the waist, try this trick. Fold a rubber band in half and loop it trough the buttonhole in your jeans. Then slip both loops of the rubber band over the button. Raise the zipper as much as you can. Wear a long, loose top to camouflage your hack.

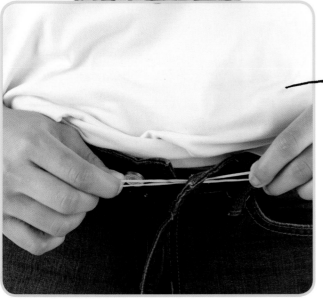

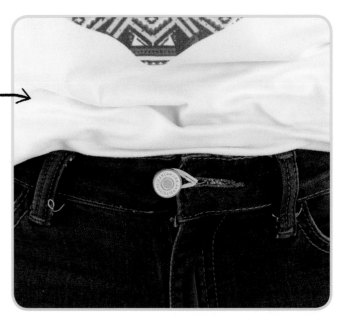

LEARN TO LAYER

Do you love layering but hate feeling like they aren't laying the right way? Try these tricks to get the perfect fit.

THE ULTIMATE LAYER TRICK

Wearing a button-down shirt under a fitted sweater can be a great fall fashion look. The crisp collar and cuffs look clean and polished, while the sweater looks cozy and warm. But there is a trick to getting this look right. Before you pull your sweater on, throw on a fitted tank top over the button-down. This will help smooth the buttons and prevent bunching so that your sweater can lie more smoothly.

SUMMER STAPLES TO FALL FAVORITES

You don't have to say *sayonara* to summer clothes when cold weather hits. Try some tricks to help you fit some summer clothes into a perfect fall wardrobe. Just layer, belt, and have fun!

Don't put your dressy shorts away just yet. Keep wearing your shorts through the fall season by layering them. Wear a pair of vivid tights underneath to instantly dress them up and make them warmer.

Ripped jeans aren't just for summer days. Get the latest look by layering your distressed denim over patterned leggings or tights.

Start with a summer dress. Add a long cardigan. Wrap a thin belt around the outside of the cardigan. For an extra touch, throw on a scarf.

No outfit is complete without an accessory or two. Accessories can be a fun way to personalize your look. Some glam earrings can dress up a simple outfit. And a slouchy scarf can turn a formal-looking top into something more casual.

CHAPTER 5

ACCESSORY HACKS

Clean Your
BLING

Is your jewelry looking a little dull? You don't need to buy an expensive jewelry cleaner to restore its shine. Just poke around your house to find these simple, surprising cleansers.

KETCHUP

Ketchup isn't just the perfect sauce for fries. You can also use ketchup to polish up your silver jewelry. Fill a bowl with ketchup, and soak your old silver and sterling silver jewelry in it. Wait for five minutes, and then use an old toothbrush to gently rub the ketchup all around the silver. Finally, rinse the jewelry clean in water. Then dry and wear!

WINDOW CLEANER

If you want your jewels to be extra sparkly, grab a little window cleaner. Spray it on your hard jewelry and gemstones. Use an old toothbrush to scrub any small cracks or crevices. Rinse with warm water and dry them with a clean rag.

TOOTHPASTE

Use a non-gel toothpaste to shine up your hard jewelry and precious stones. Spread a little on an old toothbrush and gently scrub. Rinse with water and dry with a clean rag. Do not use any of these methods on pearls. Doing so could damage your jewelry.

QUICK JEWELRY FIXES

LOST EARRING BACKS

Earring backs might not seem important — until you lose one. If you aren't near your jewelry box for a quick replacement, try these hacks to keep your earring in place.

PENCIL ERASER

Use a pair of scissors to snip the eraser off a pencil. Then use the post on your earring to poke a small hole in the eraser. Then put the earring back on, and slip the eraser on as a back.

CLEAR TAPE

Take a small square of tape and fold it several times to create a tiny square. Take off your earring and use the post to poke a hole through all the layers of tape. Then put your earring back on, and slip the tape onto the post. This trick won't last long, but it will keep your earring in place as long as you're careful.

PUT ON YOUR OWN BRACELET

Bracelets can be tricky to put on when you're alone. If you don't have someone nearby to help fasten it, try this simple trick.

WHAT TO DO:

Step 1 Unbend the paper clip once so that it looks like a tall S.

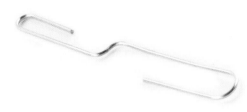

Step 2 Hook the hoop end of your bracelet around one end of the paper clip.

Step 3 Drape the bracelet across your wrist. Pinch the paper clip between your thumb and forefinger of the same hand.

Step 4 Use your other hand to bring the clasp to the loop and hook the bracelet. Remove the paper clip.

YOUR SUPER SCARF GUIDE

Scarves are the ultimate fashion accessories. They can be worn in hundreds of styles. These simple scarf knots will take your style to the next level.

FRENCH KNOT

Step 1 Use a long rectangular scarf. Fold the scarf in half and drape it around the back of your neck.

Step 2 Take one loose end and thread it through the looped end from above.

Step 3 Take the other loose end and thread it through the looped end from below.

INFINITY KNOT

Step 1 Use a large square or rectangle scarf. Tie two opposite corners together in a double knot to create a loop.

Step 3 Hang the loop over your head, with the knot behind your neck.

Step 4 Twist the hanging scarf once, and loop this section behind your head again.

TOP KNOT TURBAN

Step 1 Use a long, rectangular scarf. Place the middle of the scarf at the back of your head, and pull the two loose ends out in front of you.

Step 2 Tie the two ends at the base of your hairline.

Step 3 Twist the two ends to form a long cable out in front of you.

Step 4 Carefully twist the long end into a bun at the front of your head. Tuck the loose ends of the scarf under the bun.

TWISTED TURBAN KNOT

Step 1 Use a small, square scarf. Fold the scarf into thirds to make a long, thin rectangle.

Step 2 Wrap the scarf around the back of your head, and pull the loose ends forward.

Step 3 Tie the ends in a knot.

Step 4 Tuck one loose end over the scarf and the other end under so that the front knot looks twisted.

SUNGLASS SOLUTIONS

Sunglasses are great, functional accessories. But unlike prescription eyeglasses, sunglasses aren't usually professionally fitted to your face. Sunglasses are also often made from lower quality materials. Knowing a few sunglasses hacks can help you get more life and a better fit out of your shades.

SLIPPERY SHADES

If your sunglasses don't fit right they can slip down your nose. Get a snugger fit by looping hair ties around the bows of your glasses so that they sit securely behind your ears.

SCRATCH SOLUTION

If you accidentally scratch the lenses of your sunglasses, put a little non-gel toothpaste onto a cotton ball. Using a gentle, circular motion, rub the lens. Rinse with water, and use a clean cloth to dry it.

DON'T LOSE A SCREW!

If you notice that a screw is loose on your sunglasses, act fast! Apply a little clear nail polish to the screw to hold it in place until you can get a tiny screwdriver to fix it.

An amazing wardrobe doesn't consist of the most clothes or the newest trends. People who have the best style are comfortable and confident in whatever they are wearing. It's better to have a handful of shirts that make you feel incredible than a closet stuffed with clothes that don't feel right.

CHAPTER 6
DE-CLUTTER AND DOWNSIZE

DOWNSIZE YOUR CLOSET

You probably have clothes in your closet that you rarely wear. If you aren't getting much use out of them, ask yourself if someone else might be able to. Take any clothes you don't wear to a thrift store and donate them. Then try an experiment to see if you have other clothes you don't need.

Pick a special day, such as your birthday or New Year's Day. That day, take all of the hangers in your closet and turn them so that the hook faces out. Then, each time you wear something, return it to your closet with the hook facing in.

At the end of the year, if you see any hangers still facing out, you'll know you haven't worn them all year. Donate these clothes to a local charity or resale shop. Who knows? While you're there you might find something fantastic to add back in to your own wardrobe.

Pieces of jewelry are fun to accessorize with, but they can be hard to keep track of. If your jewelry is usually jumbled, it might be time for you to spend an afternoon organizing. After all, you can't wear jewelry you can't find. Try these quick tips to keep your best accessories in order.

Make your own earring tree by putting a small twiggy branch in a pretty bottle or jar. Hang your earrings, bracelets, and necklaces from it.

Make an earring holder out of an old cheese grater to keep all of your earrings visible and organized. You can even paint it to match your room.

If your bracelets are all over the place, stack them on an empty vertical paper towel holder. It will free up some counter space and look pretty at the same time.

Keep your necklaces from tangling up by stringing one half through a plastic drinking straw. This works whether you're hanging them or storing them flat.

SCARF STORAGE HACKS

Your scarves are useless if you never wear them. And you won't wear them if you can't find them. Try these scarf storage solutions to keep your scarves organized, visible, and ready to wear.

USE A SHOE ORGANIZER

Hang a shoe organizer on the back of your bedroom door. Roll up your scarves and store them in the shoe pockets.

HANG THEM UP

Knot your scarves along a clothes hanger and place them in a central spot in your closet.

ROLL THEM UP

Roll your scarves into neat little bundles and store them in your drawers.

SHOE STORAGE

How does your closet look? Is the floor piled with dirty shoes? Try a few simple shoe hacks to turn that messy pile into a lovely, orderly collection.

One way to keep your closet organized is to hang up your shoes. This keeps them off the floor and at eye level. You may notice that you hang up a pair of shoes but never put them on. If that's the case, save some space and donate them to a thrift shop or charity.

WHAT YOU NEED:

wire hangers

+

needle-nose pliers

WHAT TO DO:

Step 1
Ask an adult to help you use the needle-nose pliers to make a cut in the bottom of the wire hanger.

Step 2
Use the pliers to curl the ends of the hanger into little loops.

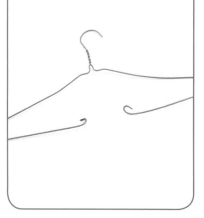

Step 3
Bend each side of the hanger into a U-shape. Now you have the perfect shoe hanger.

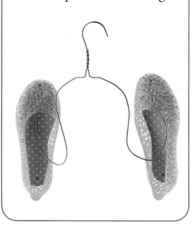

A Tip for Tall Boots
Do you go wild for a hot pair of boots? They may not fit on a hanger, but you can keep them from tipping over by inserting rolled magazines into them.

DONATE!

If you do decide to get rid of something, always donate it. This helps the environment and gives your clothes a second chance at life. Even if something looks unsalvageable, donate it. Another person might use the materials for a craft project or dishrags.

READ MORE

Corrigan, Joyce. *Marie Claire Outfit 911.* New York: Hearst, 2012.

Jones, Caroline and Fiona Wright. *Fashion Hacks: 500 Stylish Wardrobe Solutions* London: Carlton Books Group, 2016.

Low, Rachel. *Girls Guide to DIY Fashion.* Lafayette, Calif.: C&T Publishing, 2015.

ABOUT THE AUTHOR

Rebecca Rissman is a nonfiction author and editor. She has written more than 300 books about history, science, and art. Her book *Shapes in Sports* earned a starred review from Booklist, and her series Animal Spikes and Spines received *Learning Magazine*'s 2013 Teachers Choice for Children's Books. Rissman especially enjoys writing about fashion. She studied fashion history as part of her master's degree in English Literature at Loyola University Chicago. She lives in Chicago, Illinois, with her husband and two daughters.